THIS BOOK BELONGS TO:

NAME   : ....

ADDRESS : ....

E-MAIL   : ....

Date : ....

Today BTC price is : ....

Crypto traded (name) : ....

Crypto traded (symbol) : ....

Pair : .... / ....

Amount bought : ....
☐ Market order
☐ Limit order
☐ Other order type

Amount sold : ....
☐ Market order
☐ Limit order
☐ Other order type

TOTAL RESULT : ....
☐ Profit
☐ Loss

GENERAL REMARKS / CONCLUSIONS

Date : ....

Today BTC price is : ....

Crypto traded (name) : ....

Crypto traded (symbol) : ....

Pair : ...... / ......

Amount bought : ....
☐ Market order
☐ Limit order
☐ Other order type

Amount sold : ......
☐ Market order
☐ Limit order
☐ Other order type

TOTAL RESULT : ....
☐ Profit
☐ Loss

GENERAL REMARKS / CONCLUSIONS

Date : ....

Today BTC price is : ....

Crypto traded (name) : ....

Crypto traded (symbol) : ....

Pair : ...... / ......

Amount bought : ......
☐ Market order
☐ Limit order
☐ Other order type

Amount sold : ......
☐ Market order
☐ Limit order
☐ Other order type

TOTAL RESULT : ....
☐ Profit
☐ Loss

GENERAL REMARKS / CONCLUSIONS

Date : ....

Today BTC price is : ....

Crypto traded (name) : ....

Crypto traded (symbol) : ....

Pair : ...... / ......

Amount bought : ......
- ☐ Market order
- ☐ Limit order
- ☐ Other order type

Amount sold : ......
- ☐ Market order
- ☐ Limit order
- ☐ Other order type

TOTAL RESULT : ....
- ☐ Profit
- ☐ Loss

GENERAL REMARKS / CONCLUSIONS

Date : ....

Today BTC price is : ....

Crypto traded (name) : ....

Crypto traded (symbol) : ....

Pair : ...... / ......

Amount bought : ......
☐ Market order
☐ Limit order
☐ Other order type

Amount sold : ......
☐ Market order
☐ Limit order
☐ Other order type

TOTAL RESULT : ....
☐ Profit
☐ Loss

GENERAL REMARKS / CONCLUSIONS

Date : ....

Today BTC price is : ....

Crypto traded (name) : ....

Crypto traded (symbol) : ....

Pair : ...... / ......

Amount bought : ......
☐ Market order
☐ Limit order
☐ Other order type

Amount sold : ......
☐ Market order
☐ Limit order
☐ Other order type

TOTAL RESULT : ....
☐ Profit
☐ Loss

GENERAL REMARKS / CONCLUSIONS

Date : ....

Today BTC price is : ....

Crypto traded (name) : ....

Crypto traded (symbol) : ....

Pair : ...... / ......

Amount bought : ......
☐ Market order
☐ Limit order
☐ Other order type

Amount sold : ......
☐ Market order
☐ Limit order
☐ Other order type

TOTAL RESULT : ....
☐ Profit
☐ Loss

GENERAL REMARKS / CONCLUSIONS

Date : ....

Today BTC price is : ....

Crypto traded (name) : ....

Crypto traded (symbol) : ....

Pair : ...... / ......

Amount bought : ......
☐ Market order
☐ Limit order
☐ Other order type

Amount sold : ......
☐ Market order
☐ Limit order
☐ Other order type

TOTAL RESULT : ......
☐ Profit
☐ Loss

GENERAL REMARKS / CONCLUSIONS

Date : ....

Today BTC price is : ....

Crypto traded (name) : ....

Crypto traded (symbol) : ....

Pair : ...... / ......

Amount bought : ......
☐ Market order
☐ Limit order
☐ Other order type

Amount sold : ......
☐ Market order
☐ Limit order
☐ Other order type

TOTAL RESULT : ......
☐ Profit
☐ Loss

GENERAL REMARKS / CONCLUSIONS

Date : ....

Today BTC price is : ....

Crypto traded (name) : ....

Crypto traded (symbol) : ....

Pair : ...... / ......

Amount bought : ......
☐ Market order
☐ Limit order
☐ Other order type

Amount sold : ......
☐ Market order
☐ Limit order
☐ Other order type

TOTAL RESULT : ....
☐ Profit
☐ Loss

GENERAL REMARKS / CONCLUSIONS

Date : ....

Today BTC price is : ....

Crypto traded (name) : ....

Crypto traded (symbol) : ....

Pair : ...... / ......

Amount bought : ....
☐ Market order
☐ Limit order
☐ Other order type

Amount sold : ....
☐ Market order
☐ Limit order
☐ Other order type

TOTAL RESULT : ....
☐ Profit
☐ Loss

GENERAL REMARKS / CONCLUSIONS

Date : ....

Today BTC price is : ....

Crypto traded (name) : ....

Crypto traded (symbol) : ....

Pair : ...... / ......

Amount bought : ......   ☐ Market order
                         ☐ Limit order
                         ☐ Other order type

Amount sold : ......   ☐ Market order
                         ☐ Limit order
                         ☐ Other order type

TOTAL RESULT : ......   ☐ Profit
                         ☐ Loss

GENERAL REMARKS / CONCLUSIONS

Date : ....

Today BTC price is : ....

Crypto traded (name) : ....

Crypto traded (symbol) : ....

Pair : .... / ....

Amount bought : ....
☐ Market order
☐ Limit order
☐ Other order type

Amount sold : ....
☐ Market order
☐ Limit order
☐ Other order type

TOTAL RESULT : ....
☐ Profit
☐ Loss

GENERAL REMARKS / CONCLUSIONS

Date : ....

Today BTC price is : ....

Crypto traded (name) : ....

Crypto traded (symbol) : ....

Pair : ...... / ......

Amount bought : ......
- ☐ Market order
- ☐ Limit order
- ☐ Other order type

Amount sold : ......
- ☐ Market order
- ☐ Limit order
- ☐ Other order type

TOTAL RESULT : ......
- ☐ Profit
- ☐ Loss

GENERAL REMARKS / CONCLUSIONS

Date : ....

Today BTC price is : ....

Crypto traded (name) : ....

Crypto traded (symbol) : ....

Pair : ...... / ......

Amount bought : ......
☐ Market order
☐ Limit order
☐ Other order type

Amount sold : ......
☐ Market order
☐ Limit order
☐ Other order type

TOTAL RESULT : ....
☐ Profit
☐ Loss

GENERAL REMARKS / CONCLUSIONS

Date : ....

Today BTC price is : ....

Crypto traded (name) : ....

Crypto traded (symbol) : ....

Pair : ...... / ......

Amount bought : ......
- ☐ Market order
- ☐ Limit order
- ☐ Other order type

Amount sold : ......
- ☐ Market order
- ☐ Limit order
- ☐ Other order type

TOTAL RESULT : ....
- ☐ Profit
- ☐ Loss

GENERAL REMARKS / CONCLUSIONS

Date : ....

Today BTC price is : ....

Crypto traded (name) : ....

Crypto traded (symbol) : ....

Pair : ...... / ......

Amount bought : ......
- ☐ Market order
- ☐ Limit order
- ☐ Other order type

Amount sold : ......
- ☐ Market order
- ☐ Limit order
- ☐ Other order type

TOTAL RESULT : ......
- ☐ Profit
- ☐ Loss

GENERAL REMARKS / CONCLUSIONS

Date : ....

Today BTC price is : ....

Crypto traded (name) : ....

Crypto traded (symbol) : ....

Pair : ...... / ......

Amount bought : ......
- ☐ Market order
- ☐ Limit order
- ☐ Other order type

Amount sold : ......
- ☐ Market order
- ☐ Limit order
- ☐ Other order type

TOTAL RESULT : ....
- ☐ Profit
- ☐ Loss

GENERAL REMARKS / CONCLUSIONS

Date : ....

Today BTC price is : ....

Crypto traded (name) : ....

Crypto traded (symbol) : ....

Pair : .... / ......

Amount bought : ....
- ☐ Market order
- ☐ Limit order
- ☐ Other order type

Amount sold : ....
- ☐ Market order
- ☐ Limit order
- ☐ Other order type

TOTAL RESULT : ....
- ☐ Profit
- ☐ Loss

GENERAL REMARKS / CONCLUSIONS

Date : ....

Today BTC price is : ....

Crypto traded (name) : ....

Crypto traded (symbol) : ....

Pair : ...... / ......

Amount bought : ......
☐ Market order
☐ Limit order
☐ Other order type

Amount sold : ......
☐ Market order
☐ Limit order
☐ Other order type

TOTAL RESULT : ....
☐ Profit
☐ Loss

GENERAL REMARKS / CONCLUSIONS

Date : ....

Today BTC price is : ....

Crypto traded (name) : ....

Crypto traded (symbol) : ....

Pair : ...... / ......

Amount bought : ......
☐ Market order
☐ Limit order
☐ Other order type

Amount sold : ......
☐ Market order
☐ Limit order
☐ Other order type

TOTAL RESULT : ......
☐ Profit
☐ Loss

GENERAL REMARKS / CONCLUSIONS

Date : ....

Today BTC price is : ....

Crypto traded (name) : ....

Crypto traded (symbol) : ....

Pair : ...... / ......

Amount bought : ......
☐ Market order
☐ Limit order
☐ Other order type

Amount sold : ......
☐ Market order
☐ Limit order
☐ Other order type

TOTAL RESULT : ....
☐ Profit
☐ Loss

GENERAL REMARKS / CONCLUSIONS

Date : ....

Today BTC price is : ....

Crypto traded (name) : ....

Crypto traded (symbol) : ....

Pair : ...... / ......

Amount bought : ......
☐ Market order
☐ Limit order
☐ Other order type

Amount sold : ......
☐ Market order
☐ Limit order
☐ Other order type

TOTAL RESULT : ......
☐ Profit
☐ Loss

GENERAL REMARKS / CONCLUSIONS

Date : ....

Today BTC price is : ....

Crypto traded (name) : ....

Crypto traded (symbol) : ....

Pair : ...... / ......

Amount bought : ......
☐ Market order
☐ Limit order
☐ Other order type

Amount sold : ......
☐ Market order
☐ Limit order
☐ Other order type

TOTAL RESULT : ....
☐ Profit
☐ Loss

GENERAL REMARKS / CONCLUSIONS

Date : ....

Today BTC price is : ....

Crypto traded (name) : ....

Crypto traded (symbol) : ....

Pair : .... / ....

Amount bought : ....
- ☐ Market order
- ☐ Limit order
- ☐ Other order type

Amount sold : ....
- ☐ Market order
- ☐ Limit order
- ☐ Other order type

TOTAL RESULT : ....
- ☐ Profit
- ☐ Loss

GENERAL REMARKS / CONCLUSIONS

Date : ....

Today BTC price is : ....

Crypto traded (name) : ....

Crypto traded (symbol) : ....

Pair : ...... / ......

Amount bought : ....
☐ Market order
☐ Limit order
☐ Other order type

Amount sold : ....
☐ Market order
☐ Limit order
☐ Other order type

TOTAL RESULT : ....
☐ Profit
☐ Loss

GENERAL REMARKS / CONCLUSIONS

Date : ....

Today BTC price is : ....

Crypto traded (name) : ....

Crypto traded (symbol) : ....

Pair : ...... / ......

Amount bought : ......
☐ Market order
☐ Limit order
☐ Other order type

Amount sold : ......
☐ Market order
☐ Limit order
☐ Other order type

TOTAL RESULT : ......
☐ Profit
☐ Loss

GENERAL REMARKS / CONCLUSIONS

Date : ....

Today BTC price is : ....

Crypto traded (name) : ....

Crypto traded (symbol) : ....

Pair : ...... / ......

Amount bought : ......
☐ Market order
☐ Limit order
☐ Other order type

Amount sold : ......
☐ Market order
☐ Limit order
☐ Other order type

TOTAL RESULT : ....
☐ Profit
☐ Loss

GENERAL REMARKS / CONCLUSIONS

Date : ....

Today BTC price is : ....

Crypto traded (name) : ....

Crypto traded (symbol) : ....

Pair : ...... / ......

Amount bought : ......
☐ Market order
☐ Limit order
☐ Other order type

Amount sold : ......
☐ Market order
☐ Limit order
☐ Other order type

TOTAL RESULT : ....
☐ Profit
☐ Loss

GENERAL REMARKS / CONCLUSIONS

Date : ....

Today BTC price is : ....

Crypto traded (name) : ....

Crypto traded (symbol) : ....

Pair : ...... / ......

Amount bought : ......
☐ Market order
☐ Limit order
☐ Other order type

Amount sold : ......
☐ Market order
☐ Limit order
☐ Other order type

TOTAL RESULT : ....
☐ Profit
☐ Loss

GENERAL REMARKS / CONCLUSIONS

Date : ....

Today BTC price is : ....

Crypto traded (name) : ....

Crypto traded (symbol) : ....

Pair : .... / ......

Amount bought : .... ☐ Market order
☐ Limit order
☐ Other order type

Amount sold : .... ☐ Market order
☐ Limit order
☐ Other order type

TOTAL RESULT : .... ☐ Profit
☐ Loss

GENERAL REMARKS / CONCLUSIONS

Date : ....

Today BTC price is : ....

Crypto traded (name) : ....

Crypto traded (symbol) : ....

Pair : ...... / ......

Amount bought : ......
☐ Market order
☐ Limit order
☐ Other order type

Amount sold : ......
☐ Market order
☐ Limit order
☐ Other order type

TOTAL RESULT : ....
☐ Profit
☐ Loss

GENERAL REMARKS / CONCLUSIONS

Date : ....

Today BTC price is : ....

Crypto traded (name) : ....

Crypto traded (symbol) : ....

Pair : ...... / ......

Amount bought : ....   ☐ Market order
☐ Limit order
☐ Other order type

Amount sold : ....   ☐ Market order
☐ Limit order
☐ Other order type

TOTAL RESULT : ....   ☐ Profit
☐ Loss

GENERAL REMARKS / CONCLUSIONS

Date : ....

Today BTC price is : ....

Crypto traded (name) : ....

Crypto traded (symbol) : ....

Pair : .... / ....

Amount bought : ....
- ☐ Market order
- ☐ Limit order
- ☐ Other order type

Amount sold : ....
- ☐ Market order
- ☐ Limit order
- ☐ Other order type

TOTAL RESULT : ....
- ☐ Profit
- ☐ Loss

GENERAL REMARKS / CONCLUSIONS

Date : ....

Today BTC price is : ....

Crypto traded (name) : ....

Crypto traded (symbol) : ....

Pair : ...... / ......

Amount bought : ......   ☐ Market order
                          ☐ Limit order
                          ☐ Other order type

Amount sold : ......   ☐ Market order
                          ☐ Limit order
                          ☐ Other order type

TOTAL RESULT : ......   ☐ Profit
                          ☐ Loss

GENERAL REMARKS / CONCLUSIONS

Date : ....

Today BTC price is : ....

Crypto traded (name) : ....

Crypto traded (symbol) : ....

Pair : ...... / ......

Amount bought : ....
☐ Market order
☐ Limit order
☐ Other order type

Amount sold : ....
☐ Market order
☐ Limit order
☐ Other order type

TOTAL RESULT : ....
☐ Profit
☐ Loss

GENERAL REMARKS / CONCLUSIONS

Date : ....

Today BTC price is : ....

Crypto traded (name) : ....

Crypto traded (symbol) : ....

Pair : ...... / ......

Amount bought : ......
☐ Market order
☐ Limit order
☐ Other order type

Amount sold : ......
☐ Market order
☐ Limit order
☐ Other order type

TOTAL RESULT : ....
☐ Profit
☐ Loss

GENERAL REMARKS / CONCLUSIONS

Date : ....

Today BTC price is : ....

Crypto traded (name) : ....

Crypto traded (symbol) : ....

Pair : .... / ....

Amount bought : .... ☐ Market order
☐ Limit order
☐ Other order type

Amount sold : .... ☐ Market order
☐ Limit order
☐ Other order type

TOTAL RESULT : .... ☐ Profit
☐ Loss

GENERAL REMARKS / CONCLUSIONS

Date : ....

Today BTC price is : ....

Crypto traded (name) : ....

Crypto traded (symbol) : ....

Pair : ...... / ......

Amount bought : ......
☐ Market order
☐ Limit order
☐ Other order type

Amount sold : ......
☐ Market order
☐ Limit order
☐ Other order type

TOTAL RESULT : ......
☐ Profit
☐ Loss

GENERAL REMARKS / CONCLUSIONS

Date : ....

Today BTC price is : ....

Crypto traded (name) : ....

Crypto traded (symbol) : ....

Pair : ...... / ......

Amount bought : ......
☐ Market order
☐ Limit order
☐ Other order type

Amount sold : ......
☐ Market order
☐ Limit order
☐ Other order type

TOTAL RESULT : ....
☐ Profit
☐ Loss

GENERAL REMARKS / CONCLUSIONS

Date : ....

Today BTC price is : ....

Crypto traded (name) : ....

Crypto traded (symbol) : ....

Pair : ...... / ......

Amount bought : .... ☐ Market order
☐ Limit order
☐ Other order type

Amount sold : .... ☐ Market order
☐ Limit order
☐ Other order type

TOTAL RESULT : .... ☐ Profit
☐ Loss

GENERAL REMARKS / CONCLUSIONS

Date : ....

Today BTC price is : ....

Crypto traded (name) : ....

Crypto traded (symbol) : ....

Pair : ...... / ......

Amount bought : ......   ☐ Market order
                         ☐ Limit order
                         ☐ Other order type

Amount sold : ......   ☐ Market order
                         ☐ Limit order
                         ☐ Other order type

TOTAL RESULT : ....   ☐ Profit
                          ☐ Loss

GENERAL REMARKS / CONCLUSIONS

Date : ....

Today BTC price is : ....

Crypto traded (name) : ....

Crypto traded (symbol) : ....

Pair : .... / ......

Amount bought : ......
☐ Market order
☐ Limit order
☐ Other order type

Amount sold : ......
☐ Market order
☐ Limit order
☐ Other order type

TOTAL RESULT : ....
☐ Profit
☐ Loss

GENERAL REMARKS / CONCLUSIONS

Date : ....

Today BTC price is : ....

Crypto traded (name) : ....

Crypto traded (symbol) : ....

Pair : ...... / ......

Amount bought : ...... ☐ Market order
☐ Limit order
☐ Other order type

Amount sold : ...... ☐ Market order
☐ Limit order
☐ Other order type

TOTAL RESULT : ...... ☐ Profit
☐ Loss

GENERAL REMARKS / CONCLUSIONS

Date : ....

Today BTC price is : ....

Crypto traded (name) : ....

Crypto traded (symbol) : ....

Pair : ...... / ......

Amount bought : ...... ☐ Market order
☐ Limit order
☐ Other order type

Amount sold : ...... ☐ Market order
☐ Limit order
☐ Other order type

TOTAL RESULT : ...... ☐ Profit
☐ Loss

GENERAL REMARKS / CONCLUSIONS

Date : ....

Today BTC price is : ....

Crypto traded (name) : ....

Crypto traded (symbol) : ....

Pair : .... / ....

Amount bought : ....
- ☐ Market order
- ☐ Limit order
- ☐ Other order type

Amount sold : ....
- ☐ Market order
- ☐ Limit order
- ☐ Other order type

TOTAL RESULT : ....
- ☐ Profit
- ☐ Loss

GENERAL REMARKS / CONCLUSIONS

Date : ....

Today BTC price is : ....

Crypto traded (name) : ....

Crypto traded (symbol) : ....

Pair : ...... / ......

Amount bought : ......   ☐ Market order
☐ Limit order
☐ Other order type

Amount sold : ......   ☐ Market order
☐ Limit order
☐ Other order type

TOTAL RESULT : ....   ☐ Profit
☐ Loss

GENERAL REMARKS / CONCLUSIONS

Date : ....

Today BTC price is : ....

Crypto traded (name) : ....

Crypto traded (symbol) : ....

Pair : ...... / ......

Amount bought : ...... ☐ Market order
☐ Limit order
☐ Other order type

Amount sold : ...... ☐ Market order
☐ Limit order
☐ Other order type

TOTAL RESULT : .... ☐ Profit
☐ Loss

GENERAL REMARKS / CONCLUSIONS

Date : ....

Today BTC price is : ....

Crypto traded (name) : ....

Crypto traded (symbol) : ....

Pair : ...... / ......

Amount bought : ......
- ☐ Market order
- ☐ Limit order
- ☐ Other order type

Amount sold : ......
- ☐ Market order
- ☐ Limit order
- ☐ Other order type

TOTAL RESULT : ....
- ☐ Profit
- ☐ Loss

GENERAL REMARKS / CONCLUSIONS

Date : ....

Today BTC price is : ....

Crypto traded (name) : ....

Crypto traded (symbol) : ....

Pair : ...... / ......

Amount bought : ....
☐ Market order
☐ Limit order
☐ Other order type

Amount sold : ......
☐ Market order
☐ Limit order
☐ Other order type

TOTAL RESULT : ....
☐ Profit
☐ Loss

GENERAL REMARKS / CONCLUSIONS

Date : ....

Today BTC price is : ....

Crypto traded (name) : ....

Crypto traded (symbol) : ....

Pair : ...... / ......

Amount bought : ......
- ☐ Market order
- ☐ Limit order
- ☐ Other order type

Amount sold : ......
- ☐ Market order
- ☐ Limit order
- ☐ Other order type

TOTAL RESULT : ......
- ☐ Profit
- ☐ Loss

GENERAL REMARKS / CONCLUSIONS

Date : ....

Today BTC price is : ....

Crypto traded (name) : ....

Crypto traded (symbol) : ....

Pair : ...... / ......

Amount bought : ......
☐ Market order
☐ Limit order
☐ Other order type

Amount sold : ......
☐ Market order
☐ Limit order
☐ Other order type

TOTAL RESULT : ....
☐ Profit
☐ Loss

GENERAL REMARKS / CONCLUSIONS

Date : ....

Today BTC price is : ....

Crypto traded (name) : ....

Crypto traded (symbol) : ....

Pair : ...... / ......

Amount bought : .... ☐ Market order
☐ Limit order
☐ Other order type

Amount sold : .... ☐ Market order
☐ Limit order
☐ Other order type

TOTAL RESULT : .... ☐ Profit
☐ Loss

GENERAL REMARKS / CONCLUSIONS

Date : ....

Today BTC price is : ....

Crypto traded (name) : ....

Crypto traded (symbol) : ....

Pair : ...... / ......

Amount bought : ......
☐ Market order
☐ Limit order
☐ Other order type

Amount sold : ......
☐ Market order
☐ Limit order
☐ Other order type

TOTAL RESULT : ....
☐ Profit
☐ Loss

GENERAL REMARKS / CONCLUSIONS

Date : ....

Today BTC price is : ....

Crypto traded (name) : ....

Crypto traded (symbol) : ....

Pair : ...... / ......

Amount bought : ......
- ☐ Market order
- ☐ Limit order
- ☐ Other order type

Amount sold : ......
- ☐ Market order
- ☐ Limit order
- ☐ Other order type

TOTAL RESULT : ....
- ☐ Profit
- ☐ Loss

GENERAL REMARKS / CONCLUSIONS

www.ingramcontent.com/pod-product-compliance
Lightning Source LLC
Chambersburg PA
CBHW030723220526
45463CB00005B/2148